HOW TO FLY a PIPER CUB

BY PIPER AIRCRAFT, INC.

©2011 Periscope Film LLC
ISBN #978-1-935700-60-9

Foreword

This booklet is presented with the hope that it will help you understand the basic flight principles and appreciate the many benefits of flying. A series of charts acquaints you with the construction of the Piper Cub Trainer. Simple descriptions and photographs take you, step-by-step, through a typical flight lesson. If you study the charts, descriptions and photographs carefully, it will be a great help when you take actual flying lessons in a Piper Cub. You'll be a big jump ahead of those who do not understand the fundamentals covered in this booklet. We trust that "How to Fly a Piper Cub" will pave the way for your flight instruction and lead to many happy hours in the air for you.

Learn to Fly ... It's Easy, Practical, Pleasant, Economical!

 Not so many years ago flying was considered a "daredevil" sport. Pilots were looked upon with awe, planes were expensive and tricky, the cost of learning to fly was way above what the common man could afford. Then the sight of an airplane flying over your home town would cause more excitement than a good-sized fire.

The advent of the dependable, easy-to-fly light airplane has changed all this. The famous Piper Cub has brought the fun of flying within the reach of all of us. Piloting a plane is no longer an awe-inspiring art, reserved for a small group of supermen. It's easy to fly! In fact, whether you are sixteen or sixty, if you are in average good health and are capable of exercising normal judgment, you can solo a Piper Cub with as little as eight hours of dual instruction!

And, today light planes are not expensive. You don't have to be wealthy to own one, for the light plane is low in price and uses less gasoline and oil than a medium-priced car. During peacetime, with a modest down payment you can pay for a Piper Cub in easy monthly installments.

Yes, today it's easy to fly . . . and economical too!

Further on in this booklet you will find a series of photographs and descriptions that show you, step-by-step, just how easy it is. The descriptions were written and the photographs supervised by a certified flight instructor. They clearly show you how to fly such planes as the familiar Piper Cub planes shown in this booklet. If you thoroughly understand the flight principles described and illustrated, it will be a great help to you when you take your actual flight instruction. In addition, it will be to your advantage to study aeronautics at home or in school and read good aviation magazines and books. Then see your Piper dealer and learn to fly.

Learning to fly will open bright new horizons to you! You will enjoy the finest, most economical transportation of all time. In the coming air age, landing strips, small airports and seaplane bases will dot the country. Then you will be able to fly with speed and ease to the many out-of-the-way towns that are most difficult to reach by other means of transportation.

Your life will be fuller, happier and more healthful in the coming air age. For instance, you will fly to your favorite vacation spot or to an entirely new one much more quickly and more often. You'll have more time at your favorite rendezvous . . . more time to fish, hunt, swim or just loaf and relax.

And, flying won't be limited to pleasure trips. Your business life, too, will be materially affected by the coming air age. For then, in your own or a company-owned light plane, you will meet appointments, make business or sales calls, or visit your men in the field, with a minimum loss of time from your office or plant. You not only will cover your present territory more quickly, but will be able to make new, more distant calls and expand your territory considerably. You will save valuable time . . . and money too.

If your occupation is farming, you can look forward to the coming air age with just as much anticipation as your city cousins. A field can be easily made into a landing area and a barn or shed converted into a hangar for your plane. You will fly quickly to market for repair parts for your farm equipment. You will dust your crops in minutes, where it now takes many hours. When snowed under or bogged-down by mud, you will be able to reach town for supplies and fly the children to school in your plane.

Yes, flying is indeed easy, practical, pleasant and economical. Plan to learn to fly soon in a Piper Cub. On the following pages you will find three popular Piper Cub models pictured and described.

Piper Cub
Super Cruiser

The Piper Cub Super Cruiser combines a multi-purpose usefulness unequalled in any plane within hundreds of dollars of its price. Flight schools and flying service operators find the Piper Cub Super Cruiser an efficient and economical primary pilot trainer. If blind flying equipment is installed it becomes an excellent ship for instrument instruction. It can be used for night flying and solo cross-country phases by the installation of lights and battery. It's 38-gallon gas capacity, over 95-mile-per-hour cruising speed and unusual payload ideally adapt it to the Civil Air Patrol flying. Standard equipment includes a more luxurious interior with deep, comfortable, contrasting upholstery, dual hydraulic brakes and parking brake, steerable tail wheel and compass. The Piper Cub Super Cruiser is built to serve every flight requirement.

A DELUXE MODEL. Piper Cub Super Cruiser is available, during peacetime, with special paint, navigation lights and battery.

THE SAFEST,
MOST ECONOMICAL
THREE-PLACE PLANE
EVER BUILT

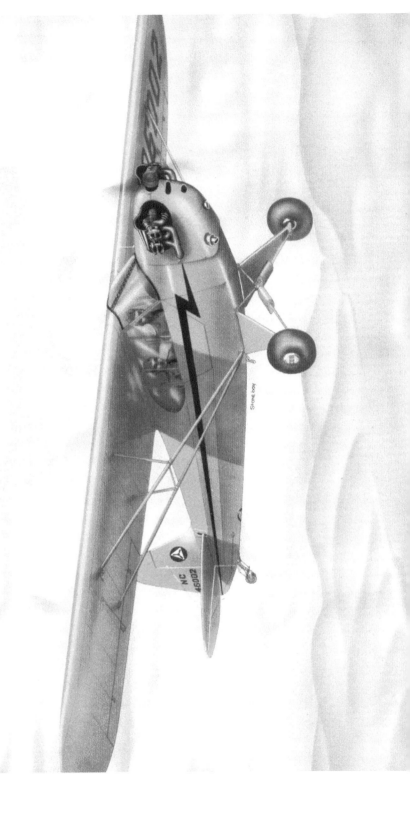

Piper Cub
Trainer

America's most widely used airplane is the Piper Cub Trainer. Easy to fly, economical to operate, low in price and easy to buy, during peacetime, on the Piper pay-as-you-fly plan. It has long been the favorite among flight instructors, flying service operators and private owners as well. In this popular trainer, thousands of Uncle Sam's pilots, in all branches of the Service, took their initial flight instruction. The Piper Cub Trainer carries two people in tandem-seating arrangement, the same as in training planes of the U. S. Army and Navy. Basically like the L-4 series military version and the Navy NE-1 training plane, it is designed with flight characteristics which make for safe handling by beginners. It is shown in use by the Civil Air Patrol, with standard color combination of Piper Cub yellow with black trim. Choice of 65 h.p. Continental, Lycoming or Franklin engines, with stainless-steel exhaust muffler and dual magneto ignition.

THE WORLD'S MOST POPULAR TRAINING PLANE

Piper Cub
Sea Scout

The Piper Cub Sea Scout brings you closer to the thousands of water playgrounds in the United States and permits you to reach in hours fishing and hunting places which require days to drive by car. It is ideally suited for Civil Air Patrol flying over sections of the country where lakes or inland waterways abound. Available, during peacetime, in the popular Piper Cub Trainer model, and having the same basic specifications, the Piper Cub Sea Scout comes equipped with the new internally braced plastic plywood floats or metal floats and regular wheel landing gear as well. Each is quickly interchangeable with the other, so you can fly your Sea Scout as a seaplane throughout the summer and convert it to a landplane for winter flying. The Piper Cub Sea Scout is completely metalized to protect all parts from salt water corrosion.

A PIPER CUB SUPER SEA SCOUT is available during peacetime, in the Piper Cub Super Cruiser model.

FUN ON THE
WATER OR
IN THE AIR

SPECIFICATIONS

General Specifications	65 H.P.* Trainer	100 H.P.** Super Cruiser
Length Overall	22' 4½"	22' 6"
Height Overall	6' 8"	6' 10"
Wing Span	35' 2½"	35' 5½"
Total Area (sq. ft.)	178½	179.3
Chord	63"	63"
Weight Empty (lbs.)	680	900
Useful Load (lbs.)	540	650
Gross Weight (lbs.)	1220	1550
Baggage Compartment	10"x10"x24"	11"x12"x26"
Baggage Capacity	20 lbs.	40 lbs.
Rate of Climb (Full Load)	450 ft.	650 ft.
Design Level Flight Speed	90 mph	110 mph
Cruising Range (miles)	206	556
Landing Speed	38 mph	45 mph
Absolute Ceiling (solo)	14,000 ft	18,000 ft
Gliding Ratio	10 to 1	9 to 1
Gas Consumption	4 gal. per hr	6½ gal. per hr
Gas Tank Capacity	12 gallons	38 gallons

*Piper Cub Sea Scout—Same specifications as 65 H.P. Trainer Plus
Plywood or Metal Floats and Metalizing.
**Piper Cub Super Sea Scout—Same Specifications as Super Cruiser
Plus Plywood Floats and Metalizing.
**Piper Cub DeLuxe Super Cruiser—Same Specifications as Super
Cruiser Plus Special Paint, Navigation Lights and Battery).

Specifications
Subject to Change

ENTIRE PRODUCTION GOING TO ARMED FORCES

Prices will be furnished as soon as material is available for commercial production.

Learning about the Piper Cub Trainer

B EFORE anyone can learn to fly satisfactorily, it is desirable to know something of the construction of the plane which will be used in flight training.

As we are discussing the Piper Cub Trainer, the charts on the following pages give you the necessary information concerning this plane.

On page 14 you will find a chart showing the "Nomenclature of the Piper Cub." This cutaway view clearly indicates the various parts of the plane and gives you the correct name for each part. When you know and understand these parts, you will be able to talk "pilot's language" about any light airplane.

The instruments of the Piper Cub are illustrated and their functions described on page 15. You can readily see how important it is to be able to read and use these instruments properly.

Page 16 covers the control system of the Piper Cub. After you have acquainted yourself with its nomenclature, refer to this chart while studying the chart on page 17, "Movement of Controls and their effect upon attitude of the Piper Cub." A working knowledge of how various movements of the stick and rudder pedals affect the flight attitude of the plane is most important. The movements shown in this chart are basic. Proper combinations of them will enable a pilot to make the plane do anything he desires—even the most complicated maneuvers.

An understanding of these charts and those on page 18 will prove most helpful in studying the illustrated flight steps on page 20 and pages that follow, as well as in your actual flight instruction in a Piper Cub. Study them carefully!

NOMENCLATURE OF THE PIPER CUB

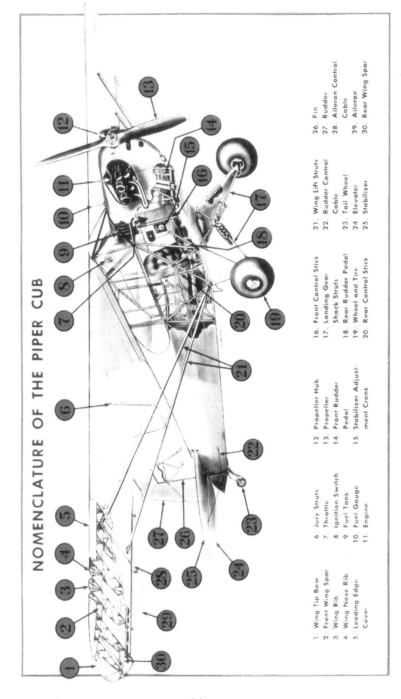

1. Wing Tip Bow
2. Front Wing Spar
3. Wing Rib
4. Wing Nose Rib
5. Leading Edge Cover

6. Jury Struts
7. Throttle
8. Ignition Switch
9. Fuel Tank
10. Fuel Gauge
11. Engine

12. Propeller Hub
13. Propeller
14. Front Rudder Pedal
15. Stabilizer Adjustment Crank

16. Front Control Stick
17. Landing Gear Shock Struts
18. Rear Rudder Pedal
19. Wheel and Tire
20. Rear Control Stick

21. Wing Lift Struts
22. Rudder Control Cable
23. Tail Wheel
24. Elevator
25. Stabilizer

26. Fin
27. Rudder
28. Aileron Control Cable
29. Aileron
30. Rear Wing Spar

INSTRUMENT PANEL OF THE PIPER CUB

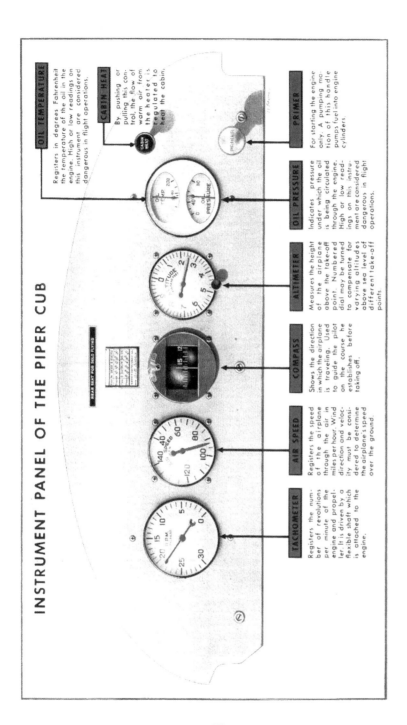

OIL TEMPERATURE

Registers in degrees Fahrenheit the temperature of the oil in the engine. High or low readings on this instrument are considered dangerous in flight operations.

CABIN HEAT

By pushing this control, pulling this control, the flow of warm air from the heater is regulated to heat the cabin.

PRIMER

For starting the engine only. A pumping motion of this handle pumps fuel into engine cylinders.

OIL PRESSURE

Indicates pressure under which the oil is being circulated through the engine. High or low readings on this instrument are considered dangerous in flight operations.

ALTIMETER

Measures the height of the airplane above the take-off point. Numbered dial may be turned to compensate for varying altitudes above sea level of different take-off points.

COMPASS

Shows the direction in which the airplane is traveling. Used to guide the pilot on the course he establishes before taking off.

AIR SPEED

Registers the speed of the airplane through the air in miles per hour. Wind direction and velocity must be considered to determine the airplane's speed over the ground.

TACHOMETER

Registers the number of revolutions per minute of the engine and propeller. It is driven by a flexible shaft which is attached to the engine.

REAR SEAT FOR SOLO FLYING

15

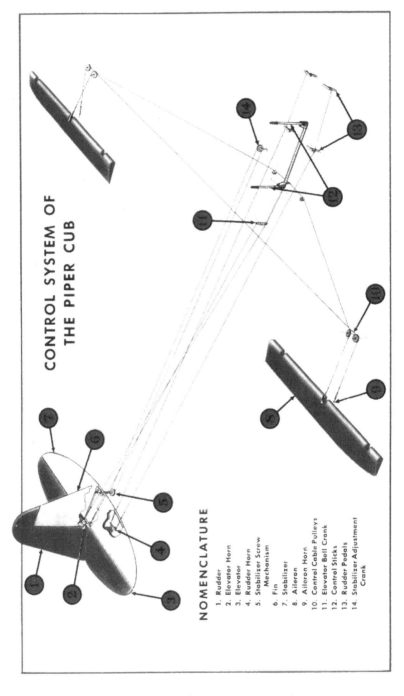

CONTROL SYSTEM OF THE PIPER CUB

NOMENCLATURE

1. Rudder
2. Elevator Horn
3. Elevator
4. Rudder Horn
5. Stabilizer Screw
   Mechanism
6. Fin
7. Stabilizer
8. Aileron
9. Aileron Horn
10. Control Cable Pulleys
11. Elevator Bell Crank
12. Control Sticks
13. Rudder Pedals
14. Stabilizer Adjustment
    Crank

MOVEMENT OF CONTROLS
AND THEIR EFFECT UPON ATTITUDE
OF THE PIPER CUB

RUDDER PEDALS NEUTRAL / STICK NEUTRAL	Result STRAIGHT AND LEVEL FLIGHT	
RUDDER PEDALS NEUTRAL / STICK FORWARD	Result A GLIDE OR DIVE	
RUDDER PEDALS NEUTRAL / STICK BACK	Result A CLIMB	
RUDDER PEDALS NEUTRAL / STICK RIGHT	Result A BANK *	
RIGHT RUDDER PEDAL FORWARD / STICK RIGHT	Result A TURN *	
RIGHT RUDDER PEDAL FORWARD / STICK BACK AND RIGHT	Result A CLIMBING TURN *	
RIGHT RUDDER PEDAL FORWARD / STICK FORWARD AND RIGHT	Result A GLIDING OR DIVING TURN *	

*These maneuvers are to the RIGHT. For maneuvers to the LEFT, reverse controls.

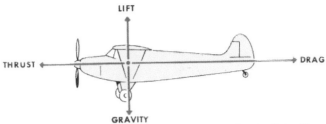

When flying, an airplane responds to four elements which affect its flight. These are, as shown above:

1. Thrust—the forward movement of the plane through the air caused by the propeller or other means of propulsion. **2. Lift**—the effect of the wing surfaces. As air passes over *top* of wing surface, a partial vacuum is created—which provides the "lift" to hold the plane *up* as it moves *forward*. **3. Drag**—is the resistance of all exposed surfaces of the plane as it is moved through the air by "thrust." **4. Gravity**—the pull of the earth *down* —the force which is counteracted by "lift" and "thrust."

THE ELEVATORS

When you press back on the stick (pull it toward you) the elevators go up as shown above. This pushes the tail down and the airplane climbs. When you press the stick away from you (forward) the elevators go *down* which raises the tail and makes the plane glide or dive (depending upon the amount of forward motion you give the stick).

AILERONS

AILERONS "NEUTRAL"   AILERONS SET FOR RIGHT BANK   RIGHT BANK

When you press the stick to the *left*, the left aileron goes *up* and the right aileron goes *down*. This makes the left wing go *down* and the right wing go *up*, tilting the plane to the left. When you press the stick to the right, the right aileron goes *up* and the left aileron goes *down*—tilting the plane to the right. When you hold the stick in "neutral" the ailerons are set to conform exactly with the trailing edges of the wings. In other words, when the stick is "neutral" the ailerons simply become part of the wings.

RUDDER

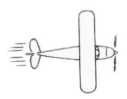  

Pressing the *left* rudder pedal makes the rudder move to the *left*. This swings the nose of the plane to the left. When you press the *right* rudder pedal the rudder moves to the *right* which causes the nose of the plane to move to the *right*.

Opposite page shows detail of the ailerons, elevators and rudder controls in the Piper Cub and how they are operated from dual controls in the cockpit.

18

You, TOO, CAN FLY!

THERE are but four basic fundamentals in good flying technique; (1) straight and level flight, (2) the climb, (3) the glide and (4) the turn. Your eight hours of instruction preceding the solo will be devoted to mastering these simple fundamentals, along with take-offs and landings.

We've seen how various movements of the controls result in different attitudes of the ship. Now let's go along with a student in a Piper Cub Trainer on one of the first flights, and actually see how easy flying can be. On the following pages we have presented a typical early lesson. Each step is clearly illustrated and explained from the beginning of the flight to its completion. Positions of the controls for the take-off, climb, glide, turn and landing are shown, and the attitude of the ship for each position. Look over these pages and study the illustrations. Then, when you step into a Piper Cub and get ready for your first lesson, you'll be familiar with the fundamentals of flight, and your instructions will be all the easier and more enjoyable.

Of course, you cannot learn flying from a booklet, any more than you can learn to drive an automobile by reading about it. You must learn to fly in the air. But we hope the series on the next few pages will show you that the "mysterious art of flying" is really something that can be readily mastered by the normal individual in a dependable, easy-to-fly Piper Cub.

1. Airplane is pushed out of hangar into clear for inspection and general check before the flying lesson begins.

2. Always check the gas by the gauge and by looking into tank. Fill the tank when necessary.

3. Check the oil by removing the cap and looking at the oil stick.

4. Place chocks securely in front of both wheels.

5. Get in ship and fasten safety belt.

6. Check rudder and stick controls for freedom of movement by moving them in all positions.

7. Push the fuel valve into the "ON" position.

8. Check the switch to make sure it is off.

9. Prop is pulled through once or twice by hand.

10. Turn on the switch to "BOTH."

11. Now the prop is swung through to start engine.

12. The chocks are pulled from in front of the wheels, using the ropes attached to them.

13. Check oil pressure gauge for normal reading.

14. Close the doors and fasten them securely.

15. Observe the windsock and S-taxi to the runway. Always take off and land INTO the wind. Do not taxi faster than normal walking speed. Look around and ahead constantly for other aircraft.

16. Near end of runway stop, apply brakes, advance throttle to 1400 RPM and check the magnetos with the tachometer. Check for other aircraft landing or taking off. If clear, proceed to position on runway.

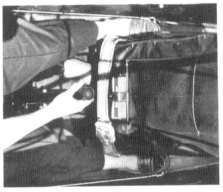

17. Ease the throttle all the way forward. After a run of about 100 feet, push the stick forward to lift the tail.

18. With tail up, in level flight position, ready to leave the ground.

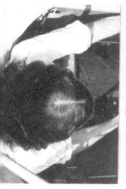

19. As the tail comes up, ease the stick back to neutral to keep level position.

20. As the ship gains speed, slowly apply more back pressure to the stick.

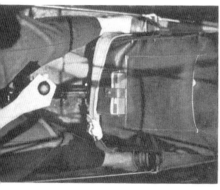

21. The ship is now airborn. Upon reaching an altitude of about 10 feet, ease stick forward to neutral to let flying speed increase.

22. The ship is in level flight, just off the runway.

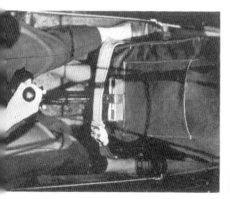

23. As flying speed increases, ease the stick back to normal climbing position.

24. Here the ship has started a normal climb, after gaining a safety margin of flying speed.

25. When an altitude of 400 ft. is reached make a level 90 degree turn to the left, with 30 degree bank by simultaneously pushing left rudder pedal and stick to left.

26. When desired degree of bank is attained, ease left rudder pedal and stick back to neutral.

27. Illustration shows ship in level turn to the left.

28. To recover from left turn, simultaneously push the right rudder pedal and stick to the right.

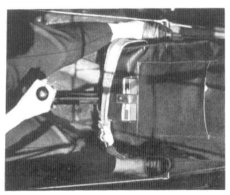
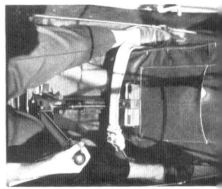

29. When ship has recovered from the turn, ease controls back to neutral.

30. Now leave the traffic pattern with a 45 degree right turn with a 30 degree bank, by simultaneously pushing right rudder and stick. When correct bank is attained return controls to neutral.

31. To recover from turn, simultaneously press left rudder and push left stick. As recovery is made return controls to neutral.

32. Then proceed to climb with throttle three-quarters full, applying back pressure to stick.

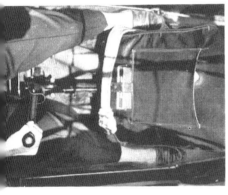

33. Now make a 90 degree climbing turn to the right with a 15 degree bank, by simultaneously pressing the right rudder, pushing stick to the right and slightly increasing back pressure.

34. Here is the plane in a climbing right turn.

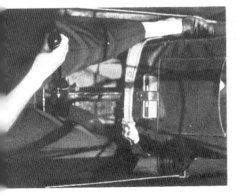

35. To recover from turn, simultaneously press left rudder and push left stick. As recovery is made, return controls to neutral, but still maintain back pressure on the stick.

36. Return stick to neutral, ease throttle back to cruising and maintain a straight and level course.

37. Now put the ship into a glide by easing the throttle all the way back and pushing the stick slightly forward.

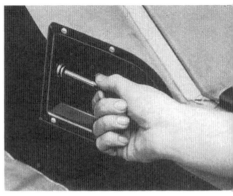

38. Always pull on carburetor heat when in a glide.

39. Ship is shown here in a normal glide.

40. Now make a 90 degree gliding turn to the right, with a 30 degree bank. This is done in the same manner as previous right turn, but the stick is slightly forward.

41. Recovery is made in the same manner as in previous right turn, but with the stick slightly forward.

42. Advance throttle to cruising and move stick to neutral. Turn off carburetor heat, make a 90 degree level right turn to approach airport pattern at 600 feet altitude at a 45 degree angle.

26

43. If the way is clear, make a 45 degree level turn to the right and swing into the airport pattern.

44. Now make a 90 degree level turn to the left as previously described and fly straight and level, paralleling the runway.

45. When parallel with the end of the runway, cut throttle all the way back, push stick slightly forward. Turn on carburetor heat and proceed in normal glide.

46. Now make a 90 degree gliding turn to the left, with a 30 degree bank, by pressing left rudder pedal and pushing stick to the left.

47. Recover with right rudder and stick to right. Neutralize controls with stick slightly forward. NOTE: Clear engine during glide by advancing throttle to cruising position and back.

48. Make another 90 degree turn to the left with a 30 degree bank, so as to line the plane up with the runway. Recover as in previous gliding turn.

27

49. When ship is about 15 feet above runway, slowly start to apply back pressure on stick to break glide.

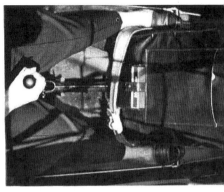

50. Continue to increase back pressure so that when ship is about 2 feet above runway the stick is all the way back.

51. As flying speed is lost, ship will settle to ground in three-point position.

52. When ship has slowed down to approximately 15 m.p.h., turn off runway and S-taxi slowly toward the hangar, watching out for other ships.

53. Turn off switch, advance throttle full forward, then close throttle. Get out of plane and push it into hangar.

A WORD OF ADVICE
FROM THE INSTRUCTOR

FLYING is fun, but to do it well you have to make it a practice to form good habits right from the beginning. Take each maneuver as it comes along and do your best to master it. Ask questions of your instructor. Practice when you're up solo. And always remember that the "hot pilot" of today isn't a death-defying daredevil. He's the common sense fellow who has learned his lessons well, takes pride in precision flying and follows the rules. Now go to it—and take real flying lessons from your Piper dealer.

FROM THE COCKPIT OF A CUB!

STRAIGHT AND LEVEL

As you sit in the rear (student) cockpit of a Piper Cub in straight and level flight, here is how the horizon looks. These pictures show normal front view as when you fly solo—with no instructor in the front cockpit.

30° LEFT TURN

Notice how, when you turn left at a 30° bank, the horizon seems to tilt to the right. With the nose in correct position for level flight the horizon line cuts right across the nose of the plane.

30° RIGHT TURN

Same as a 30° level left turn only to the right. Horizon seems to tilt to the left. In gliding turns, the nose goes *below* the horizon and in climbing turns, the nose goes *above* the horizon.

GOOD PILOTS KEEP THEIR HEADS—LOOSE!

Good pilots never have stiff necks! As they fly they are constantly turning their heads from side to side—up and down—always checking to see that there are no other airplanes near. Traffic rules of the air are strict and all good pilots fly according to them. You will be coached on these traffic rules wherever or whenever you learn to fly.

WIND DRIFT CORRECTION

When flying, never forget that your plane moves *through* the air—yet *within* a mass of air. Suppose you were in a boat on a river and the current was from right to left as shown below at left. To get to a point on the opposite bank directly across from you, you would have to row your boat at an angle against the current as shown. Now look at the picture at the right below. See? It's the same way when you fly. The wind is just like the current of a river. You have to "allow" for it—or as pilots say, "crab into it" to keep the direction you want in relation to the ground. *Wind correction is one of the most important fundamentals of flight!*

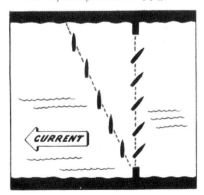 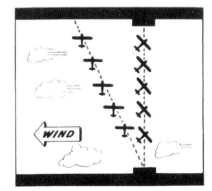

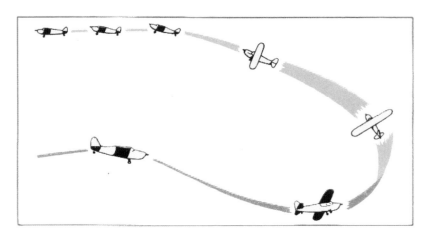

CHANDELLE This used to be called the "Castle Turn" because it was invented in World War I by Vernon Castle. It consists of a shallow dive, to gain extra speed, adding a bank of 45° and when the 45° is almost reached, applying back pressure to add *climb*. When about halfway through, the (recovery) roll out is started so that when you are heading in the opposite direction—a change of 180°—your wings are level but you are still in a climb. Then lower the nose to level flight.

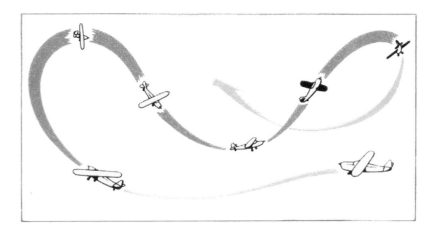

LAZY 8's These are a combination of a climbing turn, a turn over the top (like half an orange) and a turn down, with the airplane constantly changing its attitude in relation to the ground. Both the Chandelle and the Lazy 8 are known as "timing maneuvers" because they require an exact timing of control "pressures."

XPERIENCED FLIERS CAN DO

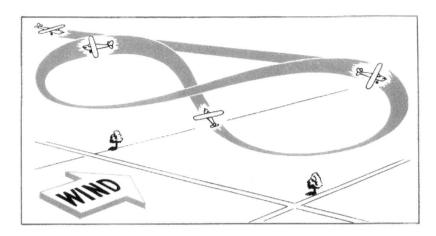

PYLON 8's This maneuver not only requires timing but takes into account wind drift because it is flown cross wind. You must stay the same distance away from the pylon all the way around, although, on one side the wind blows you toward the pylon and on the other side blows you away from it. You must use a 30° bank on the side of the pylon towards the wind and a 45° bank on the side away from the wind. Pylons should not be trees, etc., but intersections of roads or field lines.

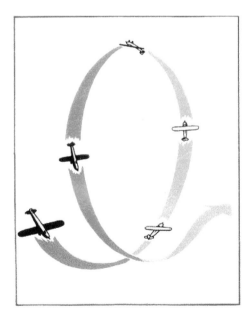

LOOP Now we're getting to where flying is really fun. To loop an airplane you first push the nose down into a dive and gain speed. As your speed picks up you must gradually close the throttle so your engine doesn't "rev." up too fast. When you have gained speed, press back firmly on the stick so the nose comes up fairly fast and when you are climbing straight up open the throttle wide. Now just hold the stick set about half way back. Don't move it back any farther. As you go over the top and start down, gradually close the throttle again. You will go under the bottom and can then level out, or pull up into a brief climb to gain some altitude before leveling out—and that's all there is to it.

LEARN WHAT YOUR INSTRUCTOR MEANS BY THESE HAND SIGNALS

1. Shakes Stick and Points to Student
Student Take Controls

2. Taps Self on Head
Student Release Controls to Instructor

3. Instructor Opens and Closes Hand
Student Is Tense . . . RELAX

4. Downward Motion of Palm Toward Wingtip
Student Bank or Lower Indicated Wing

5. Upward Motion of Palm Toward Wingtip
Student Raise Indicated Wing

6. One Finger, Circular Motion
Check Your Tachometer and Throttle Setting

7. Instructor Taps Ear
Student Apply Rudder Right or Left as Indicated

8. Instructor Points Right or Left
Student Change Flight Direction as Indicated

9. Hand Extended with Thumb Toward Student
Hold and Maintain This Heading

10. Upward Motion with Palm Toward Student
Raise or Elevate Nose of Plane

11. Down Motion of Hand
Lower or Depress Nose of Plane

12. Hand, Palm Flat, in Sweeping Horizontal Motion
Level Off or Maintain Altitude

13. Opening and Closing Thumb and Finger
Check Altimeter

14. Taps Student on Head
PLEASE Release Controls to Instructor

PIPER AIRCRAFT CORPORATION, LOCK HAVEN, PENNA.

Form No. SP45-1